CHAPTER ONE

WASHINGTON'S ROLE IN THE NATIONAL ECONOMY

The state of Washington plays a pivotal role in the national economy of the United States, with its influence spanning key industries like technology, aerospace, and agriculture. Washington's economic contributions are not only significant in terms of GDP but also crucial to America's position as a global leader in innovation, trade, and technological advancement. Let's break down these major sectors to understand how Washington is shaping the economic future of the United States.

1. Tech Giants and the Digital Economy

Washington is home to two of the largest and most influential companies in the world: Microsoft and Amazon. These tech giants have a profound impact on the national economy and the global digital landscape.

Microsoft: Founded by Bill Gates and Paul Allen in 1975, Microsoft revolutionized the personal computing industry. Today, the company is a global leader in cloud computing, software development, artificial intelligence (AI), and enterprise solutions. Its Azure cloud services are critical to businesses and governments worldwide, and its continuous innovations in AI and machine learning are shaping the future of work, education, and healthcare. Microsoft's success brings enormous revenue to the state and nation, contributing to the U.S.'s tech dominance on the global stage.

Amazon: Founded in 1994 by Jeff Bezos, Amazon started as an online bookstore and has since evolved into a global e-commerce behemoth and a leader in cloud services through Amazon Web Services (AWS). AWS is now the backbone of many digital services across industries, driving innovation in areas like big data, AI, and Internet of Things (IoT). Amazon's massive distribution and logistics networks are also a key part of America's consumer economy, supporting a vast number of jobs and services across the country. Amazon has redefined retail, logistics, and even media, making Washington a hub for innovation in these sectors.

These two companies alone have catalyzed the growth of tech startups, spurred job creation, and attracted global talent to the state. As a result, Washington has become one of the fastest-growing states in the U.S., contributing significantly to the national GDP and helping solidify the U.S.'s leadership in the global tech economy.

2. Aerospace and the Future of Global Aviation

The aerospace industry in Washington, centered around Boeing, is another major pillar of the state's economy and a critical part of America's global economic influence. Boeing, headquartered in the Seattle area for much of its history, is one of the largest aerospace manufacturers in the world and a leading exporter of aircraft.

Boeing: Known for its commercial aircraft, Boeing plays a vital role in global aviation. The company's wide-body aircraft like the 747, 777, and 787 are in operation worldwide, making Boeing a key player in international trade, travel, and logistics. Beyond commercial aviation, Boeing is also a significant contractor for the U.S. military and space programs, contributing to national defense and space exploration. Its advanced research and development in areas like autonomous flight, green aviation technologies, and space exploration keep the U.S. at the forefront of aerospace innovation.

Boeing's supply chain supports tens of thousands of jobs across the U.S., and its contributions to global trade via aircraft manufacturing underscore America's position as a leader in transportation and logistics.

3. Agriculture: Feeding the Nation and the World

While tech and aerospace often take the spotlight, agriculture is a cornerstone of Washington's economy, making vital contributions to the U.S. food supply and export markets. The state's diverse climate and rich soils allow for the cultivation of a wide variety of crops, many of which are critical to both domestic consumption and international trade.

Apple Industry: Washington is the largest producer of apples in the U.S., accounting for about 65% of the nation's supply. Washington apples are renowned for their quality and are exported globally. The apple industry alone generates billions of dollars in revenue and supports a vast network of farmers, processors, and distributors. This industry is emblematic of how Washington's agricultural sector contributes to the U.S. economy as a whole.

Wheat and Wine: Washington is also a leading producer of wheat and is home to a thriving wine industry, which is now the second-largest wine producer in the U.S. (behind California). These industries not only support rural economies within the state but also bolster America's agricultural exports, helping maintain the country's competitiveness in global food markets.

Sustainability in Agriculture: Washington's agricultural sector is increasingly focused on sustainability, adopting precision farming techniques and eco-friendly practices. These efforts align with national and global shifts toward more sustainable food systems, placing Washington at the forefront of the future of agriculture.

4. Trade and Ports: A Gateway to the Pacific Rim

Washington's geographic location on the Pacific Coast positions it as a key gateway for international trade, particularly with Asia. The state's ports, including the Ports of Seattle and Tacoma (collectively known as the Northwest Seaport Alliance), are among the busiest in the U.S. and serve as critical links in the global supply chain.

Exports and Imports: Washington's ports handle vast amounts of goods, including agricultural products, manufactured goods, and raw materials. The state's strong trade ties with countries like China, Japan, and South Korea are essential to maintaining the flow of goods and services between the U.S. and Asia, which in turn supports millions of jobs and businesses across the country.

International Trade Agreements: Washington's economy is highly dependent on international trade, and the state's leadership often advocates for favorable trade policies at the national level. The state's economic success underscores the importance of free trade agreements like the USMCA (United States-Mexico-Canada Agreement) and other bilateral agreements that promote the exchange of goods and services across borders.

5. Economic Resilience and Innovation

Washington's economy has shown resilience and adaptability in the face of global challenges, from the financial crises to the COVID-19 pandemic. The state's focus on innovation, particularly in technology and green energy, positions it to be a leader in future industries that will shape the global economy.

Green Economy: Washington has made significant investments in renewable energy, clean technology, and environmental sustainability. These efforts align with national and global trends toward reducing carbon emissions and combating climate change. Washington's leadership in this area could serve as a model for other states and nations as the world transitions to a low-carbon economy.

Startups and Entrepreneurial Ecosystem: In addition to its established industries, Washington boasts a vibrant startup ecosystem, particularly in sectors like biotech, clean energy, and artificial intelligence. The state's support for entrepreneurship and innovation is essential to driving future economic growth and maintaining America's competitive edge in the global economy.

Conclusion: A Microcosm of America's Future

Washington's diverse and dynamic economy is a microcosm of the broader U.S. economy. The state's leadership in technology, aerospace, agriculture, and trade positions it as a key driver of America's future prosperity. Washington's ability to innovate, adapt to global trends, and lead in sustainability and international trade makes it a critical player in shaping not just the fate of the Pacific Northwest, but the future of the entire country.

By continuing to invest in education, innovation, and sustainable practices, Washington is helping to build a more resilient and competitive American economy for the 21st century.

CHAPTER TWO : THE POLITICAL LANDSCAPE OF WASHINGTON STATE AND ITS NATIONAL INFLUENCE

Washington State, located in the Pacific Northwest, has emerged as a critical player in shaping the political discourse in America. Known for its progressive values, diverse population, and dynamic economy, Washington's political landscape reflects the broader ideological shifts happening across the country. Washington serves as a laboratory for progressive policies on healthcare, environmental sustainability, social justice, and technology, often pioneering initiatives that later influence national policy. Let's explore the various aspects of Washington's political landscape and how they contribute to the fate of America.

1. Progressive Stronghold and the Democratic Dominance

Washington has long been a Democratic stronghold, with its urban centers such as Seattle and the surrounding King County playing a significant role in the state's political leanings. The political landscape is shaped by a combination of highly educated, tech-savvy urban voters, a commitment to environmental protection, and a desire for social justice reforms.

Urban Dominance: Cities like Seattle, Tacoma, and Olympia are home to a predominantly liberal electorate. These urban areas are hubs for technology, higher education, and a young, diverse population, leading to strong support for Democratic policies. Seattle, as one of the most progressive cities in the U.S., often drives statewide political conversations. Issues like police reform, affordable housing, healthcare access, and LGBTQ+ rights are key political priorities for city leaders.

Rural vs. Urban Divide: Despite its overall progressive tilt, Washington also faces a pronounced rural-urban divide. While urban areas overwhelmingly support the Democratic Party, rural and agricultural regions in Eastern Washington tend to lean more conservative, favoring the Republican Party. This divide reflects a broader national trend, where urban areas are more liberal and rural areas more conservative. Balancing the interests of these diverse constituencies remains a political challenge.

Political Leadership: Washington's political leadership is predominantly Democratic. Both U.S. senators from the state, Patty Murray and Maria Cantwell, have long held their seats as part of the Democratic Party. The state's governor, Jay Inslee, is also a Democrat and has gained national recognition for his strong stance on climate change and environmental protection. Inslee's leadership has been instrumental in shaping state policies that align with progressive values, especially in areas like healthcare, education, and climate action.

2. Healthcare Reform and Progressive Policies

Washington is often seen as a testing ground for progressive healthcare policies. The state has implemented innovative programs aimed at expanding access to healthcare, addressing rising costs, and reducing disparities.

Healthcare for All: One of the most ambitious healthcare goals in Washington has been the push for universal healthcare. While Washington has not fully implemented a single-payer system like in some other states, it has made significant strides toward increasing access to affordable healthcare through initiatives like Washington Apple Health, the state's Medicaid program. The state's leadership in expanding Medicaid under the Affordable Care Act (ACA) has resulted in millions of residents gaining access to healthcare.

Public Option: Washington became the first state to pass legislation creating a public option for health insurance in 2019. The "Cascade Care" program was designed to provide lower-cost options on the health insurance marketplace by capping provider reimbursements and increasing transparency. This model is being closely watched by other states and could serve as a blueprint for future national reforms, especially as the U.S. continues to grapple with healthcare affordability and accessibility.

Mental Health and Addiction Services: In addition to physical healthcare, Washington has been at the forefront of mental health and addiction services reform. The state has invested in expanding access to mental health services, recognizing the importance of comprehensive healthcare that addresses both physical and mental well-being.

Washington's healthcare policies align with the broader national push for more affordable, accessible, and equitable healthcare, positioning the state as a leader in the progressive movement for healthcare reform.

3. Environmental Leadership and Climate Change Initiatives

One of the most defining features of Washington's political landscape is its commitment to environmental protection and climate change mitigation. Washington is often seen as a national leader in green policies, thanks in part to Governor Jay Inslee, who has made climate change a central issue in both state and national politics.

Carbon Emissions Reduction: Washington has implemented some of the most ambitious climate policies in the country, including setting a goal of being carbon-neutral by 2050. The state has passed legislation that caps carbon emissions, incentivizes renewable energy, and promotes electric vehicle adoption. Washington's Clean Energy Transformation Act (CETA), which mandates that the state's electricity come from 100% clean energy sources by 2045, has become a model for other states and nations.

Sustainability and Clean Energy: Washington's natural resources, including its vast hydropower capacity, make it a leader in clean energy production. Hydropower accounts for the majority of the state's energy, which has helped Washington maintain one of the lowest carbon footprints in the nation. In addition, the state is investing heavily in solar, wind, and other renewable energy sources, further positioning itself as a leader in the green economy.

National Climate Policy: Governor Inslee's national profile on environmental issues was elevated during his 2020 presidential campaign, where he made climate change the centerpiece of his platform. While his campaign didn't gain significant traction, his focus on climate policy has influenced national conversations, particularly within the Democratic Party. Inslee's push for comprehensive federal action on climate change has resonated with progressive leaders and activists, potentially shaping future national policies on the issue.

4. Social Justice and Racial Equity

Washington's progressive politics are also reflected in its efforts to address social justice, racial equity, and police reform. The state's leadership in these areas has made it a model for progressive movements across the U.S.

Police Reform: In the wake of nationwide protests following the killing of George Floyd in 2020, Washington passed some of the most comprehensive police reform laws in the country. The state's new laws include measures to ban chokeholds, restrict the use of tear gas, and increase accountability for officers involved in misconduct. These reforms are designed to rebuild trust between law enforcement and the communities they serve, particularly communities of color.

Criminal Justice Reform: Washington has also been at the forefront of criminal justice reform, including efforts to reduce mass incarceration and address systemic racial disparities in the legal system. The state has passed legislation to reform sentencing laws, expand alternatives to incarceration, and promote rehabilitation over punishment. These initiatives align with national efforts to reform the criminal justice system and reduce racial inequality.

LGBTQ+ Rights: Washington has been a strong supporter of LGBTQ+ rights, passing progressive legislation that protects the rights of transgender individuals, supports same-sex marriage, and ensures anti-discrimination protections for LGBTQ+ people in housing, employment, and public accommodations. The state's policies reflect a broader national movement toward greater equality for the LGBTQ+ community.

5. Technology Policy and Digital Privacy

Given that Washington is home to tech giants like Microsoft and Amazon, the state has had to grapple with unique challenges related to technology, data privacy, and regulation. These issues are increasingly important on the national stage as well.

Data Privacy: Washington has been a leader in advocating for stronger data privacy protections. The state has proposed legislation modeled after the European Union's General Data Protection Regulation (GDPR) to give residents more control over their personal information. This includes greater transparency in how companies collect and use data, as well as stronger rights for individuals to request the deletion or correction of their data.

Tech Regulation: Washington's political leaders have also been involved in discussions about how to regulate big tech companies, particularly around issues of antitrust and market competition. As Amazon and Microsoft grow in influence, Washington's role in these national conversations is likely to expand, with the state pushing for policies that balance innovation with consumer protection and fair market practices.

6. Washington as a National Trendsetter

In many ways, Washington serves as a national trendsetter when it comes to progressive policies. The state's ability to implement innovative solutions to complex issues—ranging from healthcare and climate change to social justice and technology—positions it as a model for other states and the federal government.

Policy Laboratory: Washington's policies often act as test cases for broader national reforms. For example, the state's early implementation of legalized marijuana, public healthcare options, and carbon reduction strategies have inspired similar initiatives across the country. As a result, Washington is viewed as a state where bold progressive ideas can be tested and refined before being adopted more widely at the national level.

National Influence: Many of Washington's political leaders, including Governor Jay Inslee, Senator Patty Murray, and Congresswoman Pramila Jayapal, have national profiles that extend their influence beyond the state. These leaders have played key roles in shaping national Democratic Party policies, particularly on issues related to healthcare, climate change, and social justice.

Conclusion: Shaping the Future of American Politics

Washington State's political landscape is a reflection of broader national trends. Its progressive policies on healthcare, environmental sustainability, social justice, and technology regulation are often at the forefront of national conversations. Washington serves as a laboratory for policy innovation, testing new ideas that may influence the direction of the country in the coming decades.

As America faces challenges related to climate change, economic inequality, healthcare reform, and the regulation of big tech, Washington's leadership in these areas positions the state as a critical player in determining the future of American politics. By continuing to push for bold, progressive reforms, Washington is not just shaping its own future, but also the fate of America as a whole.

CHAPTER THREE: WASHINGTON'S ENVIRONMENTAL LEADERSHIP AND THE GREEN FUTURE OF AMERICA

Washington State has emerged as a national and global leader in environmental sustainability, playing a crucial role in shaping America's green future. With its progressive policies on carbon reduction, renewable energy, and environmental protection, Washington is at the forefront of the movement to combat climate change and transition to a more sustainable economy. The state's efforts in green energy, innovative environmental policies, and leadership on climate action make it a model for other states and the country at large. In this extensive exploration, we'll examine Washington's environmental leadership and its potential influence on the green future of America.

1. Ambitious Climate Goals: Carbon Neutrality and Beyond

Washington has set some of the most ambitious climate goals in the United States. Central to the state's environmental agenda is its commitment to achieving carbon neutrality and transitioning to 100% clean energy in the coming decades. These goals align with broader national and global objectives to reduce greenhouse gas emissions and limit the impacts of climate change.

Carbon Neutrality by 2050: Washington's goal of achieving carbon neutrality by 2050 is part of its comprehensive strategy to address climate change. This objective involves reducing greenhouse gas emissions across all sectors of the economy, including transportation, industry, and energy production. The state is implementing a range of policies designed to achieve this target, such as promoting renewable energy, electrifying transportation, and increasing energy efficiency.

Clean Energy Transformation Act (CETA): One of the cornerstones of Washington's climate policy is the Clean Energy Transformation Act (CETA), passed in 2019. This law mandates that all electricity sold in the state come from 100% clean, renewable, and non-emitting sources by 2045. CETA is one of the most aggressive clean energy laws in the nation and has positioned Washington as a leader in the transition away from fossil fuels. The law sets an interim target of eliminating coal-fired power by 2025 and achieving carbon-neutral electricity by 2030, making it a critical component of the state's overall climate strategy.

Cap-and-Invest Program: In 2021, Washington enacted the Climate Commitment Act, which established a cap-and-invest program. This system sets a cap on total carbon emissions from large emitters and creates a market for companies to trade carbon allowances, incentivizing them to reduce emissions over time. The cap on emissions is designed to decrease annually, pushing businesses toward greener practices and cleaner technologies. This market-based approach encourages innovation and investment in clean energy solutions while helping the state meet its climate goals.

These ambitious policies position Washington as a leader in the national fight against climate change, and its success in achieving these targets will have significant implications for America's ability to meet its own climate commitments.

2. Renewable Energy: Leading the Transition to a Clean Energy Future

Washington's geography and natural resources give it a distinct advantage when it comes to renewable energy production. The state is a national leader in hydropower, wind energy, and solar energy, with significant potential for further growth in the clean energy sector. By leveraging these resources, Washington is helping to drive the nation's transition away from fossil fuels and toward a sustainable, low-carbon energy future.

Hydropower Dominance: Washington is the largest producer of hydropower in the United States, and this renewable energy source accounts for nearly 70% of the state's electricity generation. The vast network of dams along the Columbia and Snake rivers provides a reliable, low-cost source of clean energy that powers homes and businesses across the state. Hydropower's importance to Washington's energy mix cannot be overstated, as it not only reduces reliance on fossil fuels but also provides a stable foundation for integrating other renewable energy sources like wind and solar.

Wind Energy Growth: In addition to hydropower, Washington has made significant strides in developing its wind energy capacity. The state's strong wind resources, particularly in the eastern and central regions, have made it one of the top wind energy producers in the country. Wind farms in areas like the Columbia Gorge are capable of generating large amounts of electricity, contributing to Washington's goal of transitioning to 100% clean energy by 2045.

Solar Energy Expansion: While solar energy currently plays a smaller role in Washington's energy mix compared to other states with more sunshine, the state is actively investing in expanding its solar capacity. Advances in solar technology and declining costs have made solar power a more viable option for the Pacific Northwest, and Washington is promoting the installation of rooftop solar panels and community solar projects. These efforts are part of the broader push to diversify the state's renewable energy portfolio.

Energy Storage and Grid Modernization: A key challenge in the transition to renewable energy is ensuring the reliability and stability of the electrical grid, especially as intermittent sources like wind and solar become more prevalent. Washington is investing in energy storage technologies, such as large-scale battery systems, to store excess energy generated during peak production times and release it when demand is high. The state is also modernizing its electrical grid to better accommodate renewable energy sources, making the grid more resilient and adaptable to the demands of a low-carbon future.

By leading the way in renewable energy production and grid modernization, Washington is helping to drive the national transition to clean energy, which is critical for achieving America's climate goals and reducing dependence on fossil fuels.

3. Transportation Electrification: Reducing Emissions from the Largest Source

Transportation is the largest source of greenhouse gas emissions in Washington, accounting for nearly 45% of the state's total emissions. Reducing emissions from the transportation sector is therefore a top priority for Washington's climate strategy. The state has implemented a range of policies to promote the electrification of transportation, reduce reliance on fossil fuels, and encourage the adoption of cleaner vehicles.

Electric Vehicle (EV) Adoption: Washington is a national leader in electric vehicle (EV) adoption. The state offers a variety of incentives to encourage the purchase of Evs, including tax exemptions, rebates, and access to high-occupancy vehicle (HOV) lanes. Washington's goal is to phase out the sale of new gasoline-powered vehicles by 2035, in line with other progressive states like California. This transition is expected to significantly reduce emissions from the transportation sector and accelerate the shift to cleaner, more sustainable modes of transport.

EV Charging Infrastructure: A key component of Washington's transportation electrification plan is the expansion of EV charging infrastructure. The state is investing in the installation of fast-charging stations along major highways, in urban areas, and in rural communities to ensure that EV owners have convenient access to charging options. By making it easier for drivers to charge their vehicles, Washington is addressing one of the primary barriers to widespread EV adoption.

Public Transit Electrification: Washington is also working to electrify its public transportation systems. Cities like Seattle have already begun transitioning their bus fleets to electric vehicles, reducing emissions and improving air quality in urban areas. The state is investing in electric buses, light rail expansion, and other clean transportation alternatives to reduce the environmental impact of public transit systems.

Clean Fuel Standard: Washington passed a Clean Fuel Standard (CFS) in 2021, which requires a reduction in the carbon intensity of transportation fuels. This policy incentivizes the production and use of cleaner, low-carbon fuels such as biofuels, hydrogen, and electricity, and supports the transition to greener transportation options. The CFS is designed to complement other policies aimed at reducing emissions from transportation and promoting the adoption of electric vehicles.

Through its comprehensive approach to transportation electrification, Washington is setting an example for other states and helping to lead the national effort to reduce emissions from one of the most significant sources of greenhouse gases.

4. Environmental Justice and Equity

Washington's environmental policies are deeply intertwined with the state's commitment to social justice and equity. The state recognizes that marginalized communities, particularly low-income and communities of color, are often disproportionately affected by environmental degradation and climate change. As a result, Washington has made environmental justice a central component of its climate action plan.

Environmental Justice Task Force: In 2019, Washington established the Environmental Justice Task Force to ensure that the state's climate and environmental policies address the needs of vulnerable populations. The task force works to identify environmental disparities and recommend policies that promote equity and inclusion. This includes prioritizing investments in clean energy, transportation, and housing in communities that have historically faced higher levels of pollution and environmental harm.

Equitable Climate Action: Washington's approach to climate action is designed to ensure that the benefits of the green economy are shared equitably. This includes creating green jobs, investing in clean energy projects in underserved communities, and ensuring that vulnerable populations are protected from the impacts of climate change. Washington's emphasis on environmental justice reflects a broader national trend toward making climate policy more inclusive and equitable.

By addressing environmental justice, Washington is helping to ensure that the transition to a clean energy future is not only environmentally sustainable but also socially just.

5. Conservation and Land Management

In addition to its focus on reducing carbon emissions, Washington is also a leader in conservation and land management. The state's rich natural landscapes, from its coastal rainforests to its mountain ranges, are a critical part of its identity and economy. Protecting these landscapes from the impacts of climate change, deforestation, and pollution is a key priority for Washington's environmental leadership.

Forest Management: Washington's vast forests play a crucial role in sequestering carbon and maintaining biodiversity. However, the state is also vulnerable to increasingly severe wildfires, which are exacerbated by climate change. Washington has implemented proactive forest management policies to reduce the risk of wildfires, including controlled burns, forest thinning, and reforestation efforts. These strategies are designed to make the state's forests more resilient to climate change and protect communities from the devastating impacts of wildfires.

Marine Conservation: Washington's coastal ecosystems, including the Puget Sound and the Pacific coastline, are vital for both the environment and the local economy, supporting fisheries, tourism, and biodiversity. The state has implemented various marine conservation initiatives to protect these fragile ecosystems from threats such as pollution, overfishing, and ocean acidification. For example, Washington has focused on restoring habitats for endangered species like the Southern Resident Orcas and improving water quality through programs that reduce agricultural runoff and stormwater pollution.

Sustainable Land Use and Urban Planning: Washington's urban planning policies emphasize sustainability, with cities like Seattle leading efforts in green building, sustainable transportation, and waste reduction. The state encourages sustainable development practices that minimize environmental impact, such as promoting green roofs, energy-efficient buildings, and preserving green spaces within urban areas. These efforts help mitigate the effects of urban sprawl and reduce carbon emissions from cities.

6. Washington's Role in Shaping America's Green Future

Washington's environmental leadership not only impacts the state but also serves as a model for national and global efforts to combat climate change and promote sustainability. By pioneering progressive policies on clean energy, transportation electrification, and environmental justice, Washington is setting a standard that other states and nations can follow.

Influence on National Climate Policy: Washington's success in passing ambitious climate legislation, such as the Clean Energy Transformation Act and the cap-and-invest program, is influencing national discussions on climate action. As the federal government seeks to address climate change more aggressively, Washington's policies could serve as blueprints for federal initiatives aimed at reducing emissions, transitioning to renewable energy, and promoting environmental justice.

Green Economy and Job Creation: Washington's focus on renewable energy and sustainable technologies is also driving the growth of the green economy. By investing in clean energy infrastructure and green jobs, the state is creating economic opportunities that align with its environmental goals. This approach can help demonstrate how transitioning to a low-carbon economy can be both environmentally sustainable and economically beneficial, a critical message for America's future.

Global Leadership on Climate Change: Washington's efforts are not limited to national influence but also contribute to global climate leadership. Through partnerships with other states, countries, and international organizations, Washington is playing a role in advancing global climate goals, including those outlined in the Paris Agreement. The state's leadership in climate diplomacy, renewable energy innovation, and sustainable practices reinforces the idea that local action can have global consequences.

Conclusion: Leading the Green Future of America

Washington State is at the forefront of America's fight against climate change and the transition to a sustainable future. Through its ambitious climate goals, renewable energy leadership, transportation electrification, focus on environmental justice, and conservation efforts, Washington has positioned itself as a key player in shaping the green future of America. By leading the way in clean energy and environmental sustainability, Washington is not only protecting its own environment but also setting an example for the nation and the world.

As the U.S. faces growing environmental challenges, Washington's policies and innovations offer a blueprint for how other states and the federal government can transition to a green economy. The state's leadership highlights the importance of bold, forward-thinking action in addressing climate change and ensuring that future generations can thrive in a healthier, more sustainable world.

CHAPTER FOUR : IMMIGRATION AND CULTURAL DIVERSITY IN WASHINGTON STATE

Washington State is a mosaic of cultural diversity shaped by centuries of immigration, a tradition that continues to thrive today. With a rich history of immigrants from Europe, Asia, Latin America, Africa, and the Pacific Islands, Washington has developed a multicultural identity that plays a key role in its economy, social fabric, and political landscape. In this exploration, we will examine how immigration has influenced the state's demographics, economy, and culture, as well as the ongoing challenges and contributions that come with being a diverse and inclusive state.

1. A History of Immigration: Building the Foundations of Modern Washington

Washington's immigration history dates back to the 19th century, when waves of immigrants arrived to work in industries such as logging, mining, railroads, and agriculture. These immigrants came primarily from Europe, including Irish, German, Scandinavian, and Eastern European communities. Over time, Washington became a destination for immigrants from Asia, particularly China, Japan, the Philippines, and, more recently, Southeast Asia and South Asia.

Early European Settlers: European settlers, particularly from Scandinavian and German communities, played a pivotal role in establishing Washington's agricultural and industrial sectors. Many settled in rural areas, working in timber, farming, and fisheries, while others contributed to the growing urban centers like Seattle. Today, their cultural heritage is still evident in various aspects of Washington's cities, with festivals, neighborhoods, and businesses that celebrate their contributions.

Chinese and Japanese Immigrants: In the late 19th and early 20th centuries, Chinese and Japanese immigrants were recruited as laborers in industries like railroads, agriculture, and fishing. Despite their vital role in building infrastructure and supporting economic growth, these communities faced significant discrimination, including exclusionary immigration laws like the Chinese Exclusion Act of 1882. Japanese immigrants, many of whom established successful farms and businesses, faced internment during World War II, a dark chapter in the state's and nation's history. Despite these challenges, Asian communities persevered and became an integral part of Washington's cultural and economic fabric.

The Pacific Islanders and Filipino Communities: The Filipino community began growing in the early 20th century, with many immigrants working in agriculture, canneries, and service industries. Over time, the Filipino population expanded and became one of the largest Asian American communities in Washington. Additionally, immigrants from Pacific Island nations, including Samoa, Tonga, and Hawaii, have made Washington their home, particularly in urban areas like Seattle and Tacoma. These communities have contributed significantly to the state's cultural diversity and continue to grow.

Washington's history of immigration set the stage for the vibrant and diverse population it has today, with subsequent waves of immigration bringing even more cultural richness and economic dynamism.

2. Current Demographics and Diversity

As of recent data, Washington is home to over 7.7 million people, with immigrants making up about 14% of the state's population. The state's immigrant communities come from a wide range of countries, with the largest groups originating from Mexico, India, the Philippines, Vietnam, and China. Washington's largest metropolitan areas, particularly Seattle and its suburbs, are home to some of the most diverse populations in the country.

Latin American Immigration: Washington has seen significant growth in its Latino population, particularly due to immigration from Mexico and Central America. Latinos are the largest minority group in the state, making up nearly 13% of the population. Many of these immigrants have contributed to the state's agricultural industry, especially in regions like the Yakima Valley and the Wenatchee Valley, where they play a crucial role in fruit harvesting and other farm work. As the Latino population has grown, so has its influence in politics, business, and culture, particularly in cities like Yakima, Pasco, and Seattle.

Asian American Communities: Asian Americans make up about 10% of Washington's population, with the largest subgroups being Chinese, Filipino, Indian, Vietnamese, and Korean communities. The tech boom in Seattle has attracted highly skilled immigrants from India and China, particularly in the fields of engineering, technology, and business. Asian American communities have also maintained vibrant cultural traditions through festivals, cultural centers, and businesses, contributing to the multicultural fabric of Washington's cities and towns.

African and Middle Eastern Immigrants: Washington is also home to a growing population of African and Middle Eastern immigrants. Refugees from countries like Somalia, Ethiopia, and Eritrea have settled in cities like Seattle, Kent, and SeaTac, contributing to the state's cultural diversity and economic growth. Similarly, immigrants from the Middle East, including Iraq and Syria, have established communities in Washington, often arriving as refugees fleeing conflict. These communities have enriched the state's cultural landscape, introducing new cuisines, businesses, and traditions.

Washington's demographic diversity is not only evident in its immigrant populations but also in its native-born residents, who reflect the multicultural influences of the state's immigrant heritage. This diversity is visible in everything from the state's culinary scene and cultural festivals to its political leadership and economic strategies.

3. Economic Contributions of Immigrants

Immigrants have played a central role in Washington's economic growth and innovation. From agriculture and construction to technology and healthcare, immigrants contribute significantly across various sectors of the economy.

Agriculture: Immigrant labor is the backbone of Washington's agricultural industry, which produces crops like apples, cherries, and hops. Latino immigrants, in particular, make up the majority of the state's farmworkers, ensuring the success of Washington's multi-billion-dollar agricultural exports. This workforce is critical to the state's status as one of the top agricultural producers in the country, and policies affecting immigration have a direct impact on this industry.

Tech Industry: The technology sector, centered in the Seattle area, is one of the largest and fastest-growing industries in Washington, and immigrants are a significant part of this workforce. High-skilled workers from countries like India and China have come to Washington to work for tech giants like Microsoft, Amazon, and Google. Many of these workers hold H-1B visas, which allow them to bring specialized skills to the industry, contributing to the state's reputation as a global tech hub.

Small Business and Entrepreneurship: Immigrants are also active in starting small businesses, from restaurants and grocery stores to retail shops and service-oriented enterprises. In fact, immigrants are more likely to start businesses than native-born residents, and many immigrant-owned businesses serve as cultural hubs for their communities. Cities like Seattle and Tacoma have seen a proliferation of immigrant-owned businesses that contribute to the state's economic vitality and cultural diversity.

Healthcare and Essential Services: Immigrants play a crucial role in Washington's healthcare system and other essential services. Many work as doctors, nurses, home health aides, and caregivers, providing critical services to Washington's aging population. In addition, immigrants make up a large portion of the workforce in sectors like construction, hospitality, and food services, which are essential to the state's economy.

The economic contributions of immigrants are vast and multifaceted, with immigrant entrepreneurs and workers driving innovation, supporting key industries, and contributing to the state's overall prosperity.

4. Cultural Influence: A Tapestry of Traditions

The cultural diversity of Washington is reflected in its arts, festivals, and daily life. Immigrants have brought with them a wide array of traditions, languages, and customs, enriching the cultural landscape of the state.

Festivals and Cultural Events: Washington hosts numerous cultural festivals that celebrate the traditions of its immigrant communities. Seattle's International

District is home to festivals like the Lunar New Year Celebration, which honors the city's Chinese, Vietnamese, and Korean populations. The Washington State Fair often highlights cultural performances from Latino, Filipino, and Pacific Islander communities. Other events like Seattle's Diwali celebration and Hispanic Heritage Month festivities showcase the state's diverse cultural heritage.

Culinary Diversity: One of the most visible impacts of immigration on Washington's culture is in its food. Immigrant communities have introduced a wide range of cuisines to the state, from Mexican and Salvadoran street food to Vietnamese pho, Indian curries, and Ethiopian injera. Seattle and Tacoma boast a variety of international restaurants and markets that offer authentic flavors from around the world, reflecting the rich diversity of the state's population.

Language and Education: Immigrants in Washington bring a variety of languages to the state, and many schools and communities offer bilingual education programs to support these populations. Spanish, Chinese, Tagalog, and Vietnamese are among the most commonly spoken languages after English. Schools and universities across Washington have embraced language diversity, offering programs that promote cultural understanding and multilingualism, which is increasingly seen as an asset in the global economy.

Art and Music: Washington's immigrant communities contribute to the state's vibrant arts scene, with artists from diverse backgrounds influencing local music, dance, theater, and visual arts. From mariachi bands to traditional African drumming, immigrant communities have introduced new art forms and expressions, enriching Washington's cultural offerings. Art institutions like the Wing Luke Museum in Seattle celebrate the contributions of Asian Pacific Americans, while community theaters and galleries highlight the work of immigrant artists.

5. Challenges Faced by Immigrant Communities

While Washington is a welcoming state for immigrants, challenges persist. Immigrant communities often face barriers to employment, education, and social services, as well as discrimination and political opposition.

Legal and Immigration Status: For many immigrants, particularly undocumented ones, navigating the immigration system can be a major challenge. Washington has policies in place to support undocumented immigrants, such as allowing access to state financial aid for higher education and issuing driver's licenses without proof of citizenship. However, federal immigration policies can complicate these efforts, and undocumented immigrants often live in fear of deportation, limiting their access to resources and opportunities.

Language Barriers and Access to Services: Many immigrants face language barriers that make it difficult to access healthcare, social services, and education. Despite the state's efforts to offer bilingual services and resources, not all areas have adequate support, especially in rural regions. This can create challenges for immigrants trying to navigate essential services like healthcare, legal assistance, and schooling for their children. Language barriers also sometimes hinder employment opportunities, particularly for immigrants with limited English proficiency.

Economic Inequality: While many immigrants contribute significantly to the economy, a substantial portion of the immigrant population faces economic challenges. Agricultural and service-sector jobs, which are predominantly filled by immigrants, often offer low wages, few benefits, and little job security. This economic disparity is particularly pronounced in immigrant communities in rural areas, where agricultural work is seasonal and subject to the fluctuations of the farming industry. Addressing income inequality and improving access to better-paying jobs is an ongoing challenge for immigrant advocacy groups in Washington.

Discrimination and Racism: Immigrants in Washington are not immune to discrimination and racism, despite the state's progressive reputation. Xenophobia, anti-immigrant sentiment, and racial prejudice still impact immigrant communities. Hate crimes, racial profiling, and discriminatory practices in hiring or housing are realities faced by many, particularly for immigrants from Latin America, Africa, and the Middle East. Combating these issues through stronger anti-discrimination policies and community outreach programs is crucial for fostering an inclusive and welcoming environment.

6. Washington's Efforts to Support Immigrant Communities

Despite these challenges, Washington has made significant efforts to support its immigrant population through progressive policies and community-based initiatives.

Sanctuary State Status: Washington is one of the few states in the U.S. that has declared itself a sanctuary state, meaning it limits its cooperation with federal immigration enforcement agencies. This policy is aimed at protecting undocumented immigrants from deportation and ensuring that they can access state services without fear. While this has been a contentious issue in national politics, it reflects Washington's commitment to protecting the rights of all its residents, regardless of immigration status.

Educational Opportunities: Washington has been a leader in providing educational opportunities for immigrant students, including undocumented ones. The state's "Dream Act" allows undocumented students to receive state financial aid for higher education, helping them pursue college degrees and vocational training. In addition, many public schools in Washington offer programs to support English Language Learners (ELL), ensuring that children from immigrant families can succeed academically.

Healthcare Access: Washington has taken steps to expand healthcare access to immigrants, including those who are undocumented. Through state-level programs, immigrants can access basic healthcare services, and there are efforts to close gaps in healthcare coverage for those who may not qualify for federal programs due to their immigration status. Community health clinics across the state provide services to immigrant populations, ensuring they have access to preventive care and medical treatment.

Community Organizations and Advocacy: Numerous community-based organizations in Washington provide support, advocacy, and resources for immigrants. These groups offer services such as legal aid, job placement, language classes, and social support to help immigrants integrate into society. Organizations like OneAmerica, Northwest Immigrant Rights Project, and El

Centro de la Raza work to protect immigrant rights, advocate for policy changes, and provide direct assistance to immigrant families.

7. Cultural Diversity as a Strength for Washington

Washington's cultural diversity is one of its greatest strengths. The contributions of immigrant communities are woven into the state's economy, politics, and culture. This diversity fosters innovation, creativity, and economic growth, while also creating a more inclusive and dynamic society. The blending of traditions, languages, and ideas from around the world enriches Washington's cities and towns, making it a place where people from diverse backgrounds can thrive.

As the U.S. continues to grapple with questions of immigration policy and cultural integration, Washington's experience shows that embracing diversity can lead to a more vibrant, prosperous, and just society. The state's efforts to support its immigrant population—while addressing the challenges of inequality and discrimination—serve as a model for how other regions can foster inclusivity and resilience in a rapidly changing world.

Conclusion: Washington as a Model for Immigrant Integration

Immigration and cultural diversity have long been central to the development of Washington State, and they continue to shape its identity and future. The state's immigrant communities have contributed to its economic success, enriched its cultural landscape, and pushed for progressive policies that support inclusion and equity. While challenges remain, Washington's commitment to being a welcoming place for immigrants—through sanctuary policies, educational opportunities, healthcare access, and advocacy—sets it apart as a leader in immigrant integration.

As the nation continues to debate immigration policy, Washington's approach offers a roadmap for how states can embrace diversity as a source of strength, ensuring that all residents, regardless of their background, can contribute to and benefit from the state's progress. By supporting its immigrant communities, Washington is not only investing in its own future but also setting an example for the rest of the country on how to build a more inclusive and vibrant society.

CHAPTER FIVE : TECH INNOVATION IN WASHINGTON AND THE FUTURE OF AMERICAN JOBS

Washington State is a global leader in technological innovation, home to some of the world's most influential tech companies and a thriving ecosystem of startups, research institutions, and skilled workers. From Seattle's role as a major tech hub to smaller tech-centric cities like Bellevue and Redmond, Washington is at the forefront of the digital revolution. This position has far-reaching implications, not only for the state's economy but also for the future of American jobs. The rise of artificial intelligence (AI), automation, cloud computing, and other emerging technologies originating from Washington is transforming industries and reshaping the nature of work.

In this comprehensive exploration, we will examine the role of tech innovation in Washington, how it is driving economic growth, and what it means for the future of employment in the U.S.

1. The Rise of Washington as a Global Tech Hub

Washington State's prominence in the tech sector can be traced back to the emergence of two of the world's largest and most influential tech companies: Microsoft and Amazon.

Microsoft's Legacy: Founded in 1975 by Bill Gates and Paul Allen in Albuquerque, New Mexico, Microsoft moved its headquarters to Redmond, Washington, in

1986. Microsoft's success as a pioneer in personal computing, software development, and enterprise solutions put Washington on the map as a tech powerhouse. The company's innovations in software, particularly with the Windows operating system, revolutionized computing and established Washington as a critical hub for tech talent. Over the decades, Microsoft expanded its focus to include cloud computing (Azure), AI, and productivity software, solidifying its global influence.

Amazon's Disruption of Retail and Cloud Computing: Amazon, founded by Jeff Bezos in 1994 as an online bookstore, has grown into one of the largest and most diverse companies in the world. Headquartered in Seattle, Amazon is not only a leader in e-commerce but also a dominant force in cloud computing through Amazon Web Services (AWS). AWS powers a significant portion of the internet's infrastructure, offering cloud solutions to businesses worldwide. Amazon's disruptive business model has fundamentally changed how consumers shop, how businesses operate, and how technology is delivered, making it one of the most impactful companies of the 21st century.

These two tech giants have fostered the development of an entire ecosystem of startups, research institutions, and skilled labor in Washington, making the state a hub for tech innovation and talent. Their presence has attracted other major tech companies, including Google, Facebook (Meta), and Apple, to establish offices in the Seattle area.

2. Emerging Tech Sectors in Washington

While Microsoft and Amazon are the most well-known tech companies in Washington, the state is also a leader in several other emerging technology sectors, including artificial intelligence, cloud computing, biotechnology, and space exploration.

Artificial Intelligence (AI) and Machine Learning: AI and machine learning are rapidly transforming various industries, from healthcare to finance. Washington's tech companies are at the forefront of AI research and development. Microsoft has been a major player in advancing AI technologies through its Azure AI platform, while Amazon is integrating AI into many of its products, such as Alexa and its recommendation algorithms. In addition, smaller AI-focused startups and research labs in the state are pushing the boundaries of machine learning, natural language processing, and robotics.

Cloud Computing: Washington is a global leader in cloud computing, with Amazon Web Services (AWS) and Microsoft Azure leading the market. AWS alone accounts for a large portion of the global cloud infrastructure, offering services that range from data storage to AI-powered analytics. As more companies and governments transition to the cloud, Washington's dominance in this field will continue to grow, creating a demand for jobs in cloud architecture, cybersecurity, and data management.

Biotechnology and Life Sciences: In addition to its software and hardware expertise, Washington has become a leader in biotechnology and life sciences. The state is home to companies like Fred Hutchinson Cancer Research Center, Juno Therapeutics, and Seattle Genetics, which are advancing cancer research, immunotherapy, and gene editing. The combination of tech and biotech is driving new innovations in healthcare, with a focus on personalized medicine and digital health solutions.

Space Exploration: Washington is playing an increasingly important role in space exploration through companies like Blue Origin, founded by Amazon's Jeff Bezos. Blue Origin is developing reusable rocket technology and working on plans for human spaceflight, contributing to the emerging commercial space industry. In addition, companies like SpaceX (with operations in Washington) and local aerospace firms are pushing the boundaries of space exploration, creating new opportunities for jobs in aerospace engineering, robotics, and space logistics.

3. Economic Growth Driven by Tech Innovation

Tech innovation in Washington has been a driving force behind the state's robust economic growth. The tech sector accounts for a significant portion of Washington's GDP, and its growth continues to outpace other industries. Several key factors contribute to the state's economic strength in tech:

Job Creation: The tech sector in Washington provides hundreds of thousands of high-paying jobs, attracting talent from around the world. From software developers and data scientists to engineers and product managers, the demand for skilled labor continues to grow as tech companies expand their operations. The tech industry's multiplier effect also supports jobs in sectors like retail, real estate, and transportation, further boosting the state's economy.

Innovation Ecosystem: Washington's innovation ecosystem, driven by world-class universities like the University of Washington, provides a steady stream of talent, research, and startup activity. The University of Washington is a leader in computer science, engineering, and healthcare, feeding the talent pipeline for companies in the state. The presence of research institutions and venture capital has fostered a thriving startup culture, with many entrepreneurs launching innovative tech companies in fields ranging from AI to fintech.

Global Influence: Washington's tech giants—particularly Microsoft and Amazon—are not only leaders in the U.S. but also have a significant global footprint. This global reach enhances the state's influence on international markets, particularly in cloud computing, e-commerce, and AI development. This influence attracts foreign investment, partnerships, and talent to Washington, further cementing its role as a global tech hub.

4. The Impact of Automation and AI on the Future of Jobs

While tech innovation is driving economic growth in Washington, it is also leading to profound changes in the labor market, particularly through the rise of automation and AI. These technologies are automating routine tasks, increasing efficiency, and creating new job categories, but they are also displacing certain types of work, especially in sectors like manufacturing, retail, and transportation.

Automation in Manufacturing and Logistics: Washington is a leader in the automation of manufacturing and logistics processes. Amazon's fulfillment centers, for example, use robots to handle tasks like sorting and transporting packages, reducing the need for human labor in certain roles. While this has increased efficiency, it has also raised concerns about job displacement in sectors traditionally dependent on manual labor.

AI's Impact on White-Collar Jobs: AI and machine learning are transforming white-collar jobs as well. Tasks that involve data entry, analysis, and even customer service are increasingly being automated through AI systems. While AI is making some jobs obsolete, it is also creating demand for new roles that require specialized knowledge in AI development, machine learning, and data science. Workers in fields like finance, healthcare, and marketing are increasingly required to develop technical skills to remain competitive in a changing job market.

New Job Categories: The rise of automation and AI is leading to the creation of entirely new job categories. For instance, there is increasing demand for AI ethicists, who help companies navigate the ethical challenges posed by AI systems, and AI trainers, who assist in developing and refining machine learning models. The growth of the green economy, influenced by Washington's emphasis on sustainability, is also leading to new job opportunities in clean energy, electric vehicle development, and environmental tech.

Reskilling and Education: As automation and AI reshape the job market, there is an increasing need for reskilling and upskilling programs to help workers transition into new roles. Washington's government, tech companies, and educational institutions are investing in initiatives aimed at preparing the workforce for the future of jobs. These include coding boot camps, technical certification programs, and partnerships between universities and tech companies to offer targeted training in fields like data science, AI, and cloud computing.

5. The Future of American Jobs: Opportunities and Challenges

The tech innovation happening in Washington offers both opportunities and challenges for the future of American jobs.

Opportunities for Growth: Tech innovation creates opportunities for economic growth, job creation, and the development of new industries. Fields like AI, biotechnology, cloud computing, and space exploration will continue to expand, offering high-paying jobs and driving economic prosperity. Washington's leadership in these areas positions the state to be a key player in shaping the future of American jobs.

Challenges of Inequality and Job Displacement: However, the rise of automation and AI also poses challenges, particularly in terms of job displacement and income inequality. Low- and middle-skill jobs are most at risk of being automated, which could exacerbate existing inequalities if workers are not provided with adequate training and support to transition to new roles. Addressing these challenges requires proactive policies focused on workforce development, reskilling, and education.

The Role of Government and Policy: Government policy will play a critical role in managing the transition to a more automated economy. In Washington, state and local governments have worked with tech companies to create programs aimed at supporting workers affected by automation, including initiatives to provide affordable access to education and training. As tech innovation continues to reshape the labor market, government policies focused on equitable access to education and job opportunities will be essential in ensuring that the benefits of innovation are widely shared.

Conclusion: Washington's Role in Shaping the Future of American Jobs

Washington's tech innovation is at the forefront of shaping not only the state's economy but also the future of American jobs. With giants like Microsoft and Amazon leading advancements in AI, cloud computing, and automation, the state is a hub of technological growth, pushing boundaries in sectors like biotechnology and space exploration. The benefits of this innovation are clear: high-paying jobs, global economic influence, and the creation of new industries.

However, this rapid growth also brings challenges, particularly in terms of job displacement, economic inequality, and the need for workforce reskilling. While automation and AI will inevitably transform many sectors, proactive steps can ensure that workers are not left behind. Programs focused on education, upskilling, and retraining, particularly those involving partnerships between tech companies and educational institutions, will be crucial in navigating this transition.

Washington's approach to fostering a thriving tech ecosystem while addressing the social and economic impacts of technological change can serve as a model for the rest of the U.S. As the nation faces the challenges and opportunities posed by technological advancements, Washington's leadership in tech innovation and its commitment to workforce development position it as a key player in shaping the future of American jobs. The state's experience demonstrates that with the right policies and investments, it is possible to harness the power of technology for widespread prosperity and create a future where innovation benefits all.

CHAPTER SIX : WASHINGTON'S EDUCATION SYSTEM AND AMERICA'S COMPETITIVENESS

Washington State's education system plays a critical role in not only the state's economic growth but also in maintaining and enhancing America's competitiveness on the global stage. Known for being home to world-class research institutions, innovative educational policies, and a focus on STEM

(Science, Technology, Engineering, and Mathematics) education, Washington's approach to education serves as a model for how investment in education can fuel economic prosperity and global leadership.

In this extensive exploration, we will examine the key features of Washington's education system, its role in preparing a future-ready workforce, the challenges it faces, and how the lessons learned in Washington could help America remain competitive globally.

1. Washington's K-12 Education System: Building the Foundation

The foundation of Washington's education system begins in its K-12 schools, where the state has made concerted efforts to improve educational outcomes and prepare students for the future.

Emphasis on STEM Education: Recognizing the importance of STEM fields in driving innovation and economic growth, Washington's education system has focused heavily on increasing STEM literacy among K-12 students. The state has implemented initiatives such as the STEM Education Innovation Alliance, which aims to create more opportunities for students to engage with STEM subjects through hands-on learning, partnerships with local businesses, and specialized STEM programs in schools. This focus helps prepare students for the high-tech industries that dominate Washington's economy, including software development, aerospace, and biotechnology.

Career and Technical Education (CTE): In addition to STEM education, Washington's education system places a strong emphasis on career and technical education. CTE programs in Washington high schools provide students with practical, job-ready skills in areas like computer science, engineering, healthcare, and manufacturing. These programs often partner with local industries to offer students internships and apprenticeships, helping them gain real-world experience and enter the workforce with competitive skills.

Equity in Education: Washington has also made strides in addressing educational equity. Recognizing the importance of providing all students with equal access to high-quality education, the state has implemented policies to close achievement gaps among students from diverse socioeconomic backgrounds. Programs such as Learning Assistance Programs (LAP) and Title I funding focus on supporting schools with high concentrations of low-income students, ensuring that these students have access to the resources they need to succeed academically.

2. Higher Education in Washington: Fueling Innovation and Economic Growth

Washington's higher education system is a crucial driver of the state's economic competitiveness. Home to world-class universities and colleges, the state is a leader in producing highly skilled graduates who contribute to key industries such as technology, aerospace, and healthcare.

University of Washington (UW): The University of Washington, based in Seattle, is one of the top public research universities in the U.S. and plays a central role in the state's innovation ecosystem. UW is renowned for its research in fields such as computer science, engineering, and medicine. It collaborates closely with tech giants like Microsoft and Amazon, as well as with startups and venture capital firms, to foster innovation and entrepreneurship. The university's Paul G. Allen School of Computer Science & Engineering is one of the most prestigious computer science programs in the country, producing graduates who lead in the tech industry.

Washington State University (WSU): Washington State University, based in Pullman, is another key player in higher education. WSU is known for its strengths in agricultural research, engineering, and veterinary medicine. It plays a critical role in supporting Washington's agricultural sector, particularly in precision agriculture and sustainable farming practices. WSU's Voiland College of Engineering and Architecture is also contributing to the state's leadership in engineering and technological innovation.

Community and Technical Colleges: Washington's network of community and technical colleges plays a vital role in workforce development. These institutions provide accessible education and training programs for students looking to enter the workforce quickly or transition to four-year universities. Many community colleges in Washington have strong partnerships with local industries, offering programs in fields like information technology, healthcare, and advanced manufacturing. This flexibility allows the state to rapidly respond to shifts in industry demand and ensure that workers have the skills needed to thrive in a changing economy.

3. Addressing Skills Gaps: Preparing for the Future of Work

While Washington's education system is one of the strongest in the nation, it also faces the challenge of addressing skills gaps in the workforce. As technology advances rapidly, many industries require workers with specialized skills in areas such as AI, data science, and cloud computing. Washington's education system has taken proactive steps to address these gaps.

Expanding Access to Computer Science Education: Recognizing the growing demand for tech skills, Washington has made significant investments in expanding access to computer science education at all levels. The state has implemented the Computer Science for All initiative, which aims to ensure that all K-12 students have the opportunity to learn computer science. This initiative includes professional development for teachers, updated curricula, and partnerships with local tech companies to provide students with real-world experience.

Workforce Retraining Programs: Washington's education system also focuses on reskilling and upskilling workers who may be displaced by automation and technological advancements. Programs like Washington's Workforce Retraining Initiative offer financial aid and support for workers looking to transition into high-demand fields such as healthcare, technology, and advanced manufacturing. These programs are essential for ensuring that workers are not left behind in the rapidly changing economy.

Public-Private Partnerships: Washington's education system has also benefited from strong public-private partnerships that bridge the gap between education and industry. Tech companies like Microsoft and Amazon have partnered with universities and community colleges to develop specialized training programs that align with the needs of the industry. For example, Microsoft's TechSpark program provides support for rural communities in Washington to access digital skills training and expand broadband infrastructure, helping to reduce the digital divide and prepare workers for tech jobs.

4. Challenges Facing Washington's Education System

Despite its many strengths, Washington's education system faces several challenges that could impact the state's long-term competitiveness and the broader competitiveness of the U.S.

Funding Inequities: One of the key challenges facing Washington's education system is funding inequity, particularly in K-12 schools. The state relies heavily on local property taxes to fund education, which can lead to disparities in resources between wealthy and low-income districts. While the state government has made efforts to address this issue, particularly after the McCleary Decision (a landmark court ruling mandating increased state funding for education), disparities remain. These funding inequities can limit opportunities for students in underfunded schools, particularly in rural and low-income areas.

Teacher Shortages: Like many states, Washington is facing a shortage of qualified teachers, particularly in high-demand subjects such as math, science, and special education. This shortage can negatively impact student outcomes and make it more difficult for the state to meet its ambitious goals for STEM education. Addressing teacher shortages through better pay, professional development, and recruitment efforts will be critical to maintaining the quality of education in the state.

Access to Higher Education: While Washington's higher education system is a key driver of economic growth, access to higher education remains a challenge for many students, particularly those from low-income and marginalized communities. The rising cost of tuition and the burden of student debt can limit opportunities for students to pursue degrees in high-demand fields. Expanding access to financial aid and reducing the cost of higher education will be essential for ensuring that all students have the opportunity to contribute to Washington's economy.

5. Washington's Role in Enhancing America's Global Competitiveness

The strengths and challenges of Washington's education system have broader implications for America's global competitiveness. In an increasingly interconnected world, the ability of the U.S. to innovate and lead in fields like technology, healthcare, and manufacturing depends heavily on the quality of its education system.

Driving Innovation and Economic Growth: Washington's focus on STEM education, research, and public-private partnerships has helped the state become a leader in tech innovation, which has, in turn, contributed to America's global economic competitiveness. The innovations produced by Washington's tech companies, research institutions, and startups drive growth not only in the U.S. but around the world. By investing in education and workforce development, Washington ensures that its residents are equipped with the skills needed to lead in the industries of the future.

A Model for Educational Reform: Washington's education system can serve as a model for other states looking to improve educational outcomes and enhance workforce development. The state's emphasis on STEM, career and technical education, and equitable access to education provides valuable lessons for how the U.S. can better prepare its workforce for the challenges and opportunities of the 21st century.

Fostering a Culture of Lifelong Learning: One of the key lessons from Washington's education system is the importance of fostering a culture of lifelong learning. As technology continues to evolve, workers will need to continually update their skills to stay competitive in the job market. Washington's emphasis on reskilling and upskilling through community colleges and workforce training programs offers a blueprint for how the U.S. can ensure that its workforce remains adaptable and resilient in the face of change.

6. Conclusion: Education as a Key to American Competitiveness

Washington's education system is a critical driver of the state's economic success and plays a key role in ensuring that America remains competitive on the global stage. Through a focus on STEM education, public-private partnerships, and workforce development, Washington is preparing its students and workers for the jobs of the future. However, challenges such as funding inequities, teacher shortages, and access to higher education must be addressed to ensure that the benefits of Washington's education system are widely shared.

As the U.S. looks to maintain its global leadership in innovation, technology, and economic growth, the lessons from Washington's education system provide valuable insights. By investing in education, addressing disparities, and preparing a future-ready workforce, Washington exemplifies how a state can enhance its own economic prospects while contributing to the nation's competitiveness.

Key Takeaways:

1. STEM and Workforce Preparation: Washington's emphasis on STEM education and career and technical training helps equip students with the skills needed for high-demand jobs. This focus not only supports the state's key industries but also serves as a model for national education strategies aimed at fostering innovation and economic growth.

2. Public-Private Partnerships: Effective collaboration between educational institutions and industry leaders drives innovation and ensures that educational programs align with real-world job requirements. Washington's partnerships between universities, tech companies, and community colleges highlight the importance of these alliances in preparing a skilled workforce.

3. Addressing Challenges: To sustain its educational and economic success, Washington must continue to address challenges such as funding inequities, teacher shortages, and access to higher education. Ensuring that all students have equal opportunities to succeed is crucial for maintaining the state's competitive edge.

4. Lifelong Learning: Emphasizing lifelong learning and reskilling is essential in an era of rapid technological change. Washington's initiatives in workforce retraining and career development offer a framework for how to support workers in adapting to new industries and evolving job markets.

By leveraging its strengths and addressing its challenges, Washington State not only enhances its own economic prospects but also sets an example for how education can be a driving force behind national competitiveness. As the U.S. navigates the complexities of a global economy, Washington's approach to education provides a valuable blueprint for fostering a resilient, innovative, and skilled workforce.

9 798339 626367